SPEED CLEANING FOR THE PROS

*How to Achieve Perfect
Maintenance Cleaning*

By Jeff Campbell
with Debbie Sardone

SPEED CLEANING FOR THE PROS

How to Achieve Perfect Maintenance Cleaning

**By Jeff Campbell
with Debbie Sardone**

Table of Contents

INTRODUCTION

SPEED CLEANING For The Pros

Congratulations on your decision to become a professional housecleaner! This book will help you become a very skilled professional. It will make housecleaning something you can be proud of. If you put into practice everything you learn from this book, you'll be better than 99% of all the mediocre housecleaners in the country.

What is Perfect Maintenance Cleaning (PMC)? It's the very first complete set of instructions on cleaning houses in the smartest way possible for professionals, adapted from the book Speed Cleaning. The principles are identical but the emphasis is on *maintaining* the home using a *perfect* system, which helps to insure consistent results. PMC has been practiced by professional cleaners for over 30 years and has been perfected over time. The result of PMC in a professional cleaning company is a *perfect maintenance system.* Note we said that it is a "system." The system is perfect, even though people are not. When the principles of PMC are followed completely you get a *perfect maintenance system.* The emphasis is on "MAINTENANCE" rather than on "PERFECT". No job will ever be perfect because people are not perfect. But this system is

perfect, and the more closely you follow the PMC system the more likely you are to excel and succeed on the job. PMC is not a collection of "tips." You can't learn anything from tips—you need a comprehensive system that tells you where to start, what to do first, what to do second, and exactly how to proceed with each cleaning step until the job is complete.

PMC is not a collection of "suggestions". PMC techniques are not suggestions. PMC is a precise step-by-step method that must be followed exactly. Just as a surgeon first learns how to open a chest to operate on a heart, he or she then follows those precise and proven methods exactly. No guessing, no deviation from what he or she learned, no risking failure or death by changing what is proven to work. PMC is a proven system, and quality and consistency is the result.

Don't worry, PMC is not difficult and in fact, it makes your job easier and more satisfying. It's more fun to know exactly how to do your work and it's more satisfying to be able to be very good at your job. You probably know that sinking feeling you get when you're expected to complete a task but you don't know how to do it. It's difficult to get the results you want from a computer if you don't know which buttons to push. But, once you learn how to operate the computer program, you feel a lot better about it. It's the same with housecleaning. *PMC* teaches you new skills. Learning how to clean (or do anything else) the very best possible way can change how you feel about the activity and about yourself. As you get better and better at a task you move closer to the cutting edge of your attention. (Just watch someone play a computer game.) As you get closer to that edge, it's nearly impossible to dislike what you're doing. When you learn how to shave off unnecessary steps, motions, and repetition, you'll move closer and closer to full attention. You're going to learn PMC and one of the benefits will be to make your housecleaning job more successful and enjoyable.

PMC comes from following the Speed Cleaning system, but it's not just about "speed". We're not going to teach you to hurry up or teach you to race through your cleaning jobs. We're not going to focus on speed at all. What "Speed" means in this case is: not wasting time and not wasting effort and motion. PMC is about efficiency. When you know how to do something efficiently, you don't waste time and energy. You don't have to re-clean areas because you cleaned them in the wrong sequence. When you don't waste motions and effort, something wonderful happens — you don't get as tired doing the work. It's a win-win situation. PMC allows you to do the cleaning well and to do it as quickly as humanly possible while insuring quality, consistency, and promoting care to reduce accidents and breakage.

PMC is an intentional, planned, purposeful way to move around the house as it is cleaned. PMC also makes cleaning predictable because you will know how to clean even when the houses you clean differ greatly in appearance, size and furnishings. The result is quality and consistency.

Why do you need the PMC system? Housecleaning is an active job and PMC saves energy. It is also good for you. That's right. Physical exercise increases chemicals in your brain called endorphins. Endorphins release hormones that make you feel good. So not only are you working and making a living as a cleaning professional, but you are staying fit and keeping in shape. You are improving your cardiovascular system by working: toning muscles, burning calories and yes, losing weight while you work — talk about a job perk!

PMC allows you to please your cleaning customers, which in turn pleases your boss. When everyone is happy, you establish repetitive customers, making your job easier and more predictable. Most of us like easy and predictable!! Who wants difficult and unknown?

PMC will help you reach your earning potential with your cleaning company because when you know how to please your boss, you're more likely to get raises!

PMC helps you define your goals. When you understand how to do the job correctly, you can more easily formulate and achieve your goals.

PMC makes the job easier and gives you more confidence. When you know exactly how to do your job, your job is more rewarding.

Benefits of PMC. Besides the reasons already mentioned, you get job security with PMC. Being the best means that you are exceptional, highly valued. Also, many jobs don't give you positive reinforcement any more. By contrast, housecleaning offers a much more direct payoff. First the house was dirty and now it's clean, and whoever did it gets all the credit. You have the opportunity to be that person. Most of us don't stop to gloat over every item that gets cleaned, but each new bit of cleanliness provides a dose of straightforward positive feedback — the kind that's becoming increasingly rare. With professional housecleaning you see the results of your work instantly. When you arrive, the house may be a mess and when you leave it's beautiful, thanks to you.

Also, you cannot imagine how nice it feels to be the solution to someone else's problem! The clients will be very appreciative of your efforts. And when you get paid, they become the solution to *your* problem. And of course, the sense of pride you will feel is very real. Although physically rigorous, this work is truly rewarding and personally gratifying.

After learning PMC: You have happy customers that appreciate all that you do to make their life easier. You have a happy boss because of all the happy customers. You have a happy YOU with a full schedule of customers that maximizes your income potential.

You may be a bit nervous about learning a new skill. That's normal and natural. One way to combat nervousness is to ask a question when you have one. The more you're sure of what you're learning, the more confident you'll be. Don't guess! Ask! As with most jobs, the first few weeks are the most difficult. But the first few weeks pass and as they do, you gain skills, you learn more each day and because of that, the job gets easier and easier.

PMC is actually just 1 of 3 types of housecleaning that goes on in most households. PMC focuses on the weekly or every other week cleaning that most of your company's customers hired you to do. PMC is a thorough cleaning of a home's kitchen and bathrooms, including washing the floors in those rooms, plus dusting and vacuuming the rest of the house. Many people call this kind of cleaning Maintenance Cleaning. By learning to be an expert Speed Cleaner, you'll soon be performing "Perfect Maintenance Cleaning". They are essentially one in the same.

In addition to "Maintenance Cleaning", there is "Spring Cleaning" (or Occasional Cleaning). Spring Cleaning may include washing windows or walls or ceilings. Also hand-wiping baseboards or blinds, perhaps cleaning inside the refrigerator or the oven. The definition of Spring Cleaning can be different for different people, but make sure you ask if you're not sure if something is Spring Cleaning or Maintenance Cleaning.

The 3rd type of cleaning is Daily Cleaning. This is putting the dirty dishes into the dishwasher, washing the pots and pans, putting dirty clothes into the washing machine, folding the clothes from the dryer, recycling paper, glass and aluminum and so forth. Obviously, it's difficult for a housecleaner to do the Weekly Cleaning (maintenance) if no one is doing the Daily Cleaning. Once again, be sure to ask if you're unclear whether a cleaning task is "Maintenance Cleaning" or Daily Cleaning.

While you're likely to spend most of your time doing Maintenance Cleaning, you may be expected to help on Spring Cleaning or Daily Cleaning jobs. These jobs use a much different technique than the PMC system so it's important that you know which is which. Remember, you're learning Maintenance Cleaning (using the PMC system) in this book. Spring Cleaning and Daily Cleaning will be taught to you later.

Chapter 1.

THE PMC RULES

Here are your new trade secrets. Observe every one of them - every single time you clean.

1. Make every move count. This means work your way around the room once. Don't backtrack. It also means you must carry your equipment and supplies with you so you don't make dozens of time-wasting trips back and forth across the room. Walk around the room once and, except for the floor, you're done. It is unbelievable the time and energy you will save.

2. Use the right tools. Ah! Here's probably the biggest timesaver of the bunch. You need real tools that cut time to shreds. Most of all, you need a *cleaning apron* to hang tools on and to transport cleaning supplies as you move around the room. The method depends on it, and soon you'll feel lost without yours.

3. Work from top to bottom. Always. Period. Also work to the right and from back to front.

4. If it isn't dirty, don't over-clean it. For example, vertical surfaces are almost never as dirty as horizontal surfaces. Upper shelves and molding have less dust than lower ones. Often all that's dirty about a surface is a few fingerprints, so don't clean the whole area. This rule is not an excuse to skip cleaning something that you should clean; instead you're learning to work smarter not harder.

5. Don't rinse or wipe a surface before it's clean. You'll just have to start over. In other words, when you're cleaning a surface, don't rinse or wipe just to see if you're done. If you were wrong, you'll have to start over again. Learn to check as you're cleaning by "seeing through" the gunk to the surface below. Then you can tell when it's dislodged and ready to be wiped or rinsed . . . *once!*

6. Don't keep working after it's clean. Once you've reached square one, *stop.* Save your energy, rinse or wipe and move on.

7. If what you're doing isn't working, then shift to a heavier-duty cleaner or tool. You're going to get very good at knowing what tool or product to use. You'll be learning to anticipate what to reach for *before* you start a task so you won't have to shift.

8. Keep your tools in impeccable shape. Take care of the products that your company issues to you. Take care when you're in a customer's home so that you don't spill them or use them on the wrong surface. Make sure you get a replacement item when the one you have is worn out.

9. Repetition makes for smoother moves. Always put your tools back in the same place in your apron. You can't spare the time to fumble around for them and it's the most efficient way to clean.

10. Pay attention. Almost everything else will fall into place if you do.

11. Keep track of your time. Get a little faster every time—by following these rules—NOT by hurrying or rushing. Hurrying and/or rushing will result in poor cleaning, accidents or breakage, leading to customer complaints.

 12. Use both hands. Your work force is half idle if one hand is doing all the work. Finish one step with one hand and start the next step with the other. Or, wipe with one hand while the other steadies the object.

13. If there are more than one of you, work as a team. If your partner gets done ten minutes faster, the *team* gets done ten minutes faster. And that is a wonderful thing. You can't stop being vigilant for one moment about what will speed up or slow down your partner's progress. If your company doesn't work in teams, don't  worry. Maintenance/PMC works exactly the same with individual cleaners. Clean it once, clean it well and move on to the next task.

Like any new skill, Maintenance/PMC must be learned, practiced, reviewed, and perfected. It's worth it. The payoff is that you will clean more expertly, make more money, have more energy at the end of the day, and make your clients feel good about their home and what you've done for them.

These are the basics. The rest of the book consists of specialized sections on tools and jobs. Read the following chapter on tools and products. After that, if you're going to clean the kitchen, you are the "Kitchen Person," so you should read the kitchen chapter next. The "Bathroom Person" and "Duster" should read the bathroom chapter and the dusting chapter respectively. If you are working alone, read the kitchen chapter after Chapter 2 (Tools and Supplies).

Chapter 2..

TOOLS AND SUPPLIES

Your company will supply you with the proper tools and supplies. Your company may not have the exact same products as listed below. That's fine. Maintenance/PMC works the exact same way with other products. After you're equipped with them, guard against the entire PMC process being slowly sabotaged because of tools wearing out or supplies running low.

Cleaning apron. Nothing makes sense in this system without an apron. It saves more time than all the other products combined. It carries the supplies and tools that allow you to "walk around the room once and you're done" (see Rule 1). The apron is your friend. *Wear it*

when cleaning—start to finish. Always put the same sprayer back in the same loops and other supplies back in the same pockets after each use. Your Cleaning Apron has seven pockets, three of which are dedicated to the following tools:

 Toothbrush. Actually not recommended for your teeth at all, but it's the handiest brush for *getting into* tight places fast—like the areas around faucet handles, tile grout, impossible nooks and crannies on stovetops, light switches, etc. You'll be amazed at how often a spot will not respond to wiping but will come right up when agitated with a brush and a cleaning agent like Red Juice. This is a serious cleaning tool—not an old toothbrush.

 Razor-blade holder. It's great for soap scum on shower doors, paint splatters on glass, and baked-on food on oven windows and surfaces of appliances. It has a three-position blade for added safety. As mentioned, if your company doesn't carry a razor blade in a holder, that's fine. There is always more than one way to remove difficult-to-clean spots, etc. Never add unauthorized tools to your caddy, seek permission first!

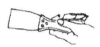 **Plastic Scraper.** Occasionally you will encounter dried-on globs that are difficult to remove with the toothbrush—like petrified lumps of pancake batter on a kitchen counter. They can be removed in seconds with a scraper, while scrubbing them with red Juice and a cleaning cloth takes much longer and is harder work.

A fourth pocket is used as a temporary storage for debris you encounter while cleaning. It is lined with a plastic insert for ease of emptying.

Carryall tray. Storage for cleaning supplies that aren't in your apron and for transporting supplies between houses.

 Red Juice (in a spray bottle). Heavy-duty or All-Purpose liquid cleaner. Professional cleaners call it "Red Juice" because the commercial concentrate often is red. Retail products include 409, Fantastik, and similar spray-on liquid cleaners. For simplicity's sake, we're going to call it "Red Juice" in this book. Use it for all spray-and-wipe jobs except glass.

Blue Juice (in a spray bottle). Light-duty liquid cleaner. Similarly, most professional light-duty liquid cleaners happen to be blue. Consumer products include Windex or any similar liquid cleaner. Use it to spray and wipe mirrors, window glass, and picture glass (but not "window cleaning" per say, other than a spot or two as needed).

Bleach (in a spray bottle). Use it to remove mold and mildew in the bathroom. (Your company may not use bleach, and that's fine). If you do use bleach, please be aware that a single drop of bleach on a customer's carpet will make a bleached spot that could cause your company to have to replace the customer's entire carpet. Please don't forget this.

Tile Cleaner (in a squirt bottle). Liquid tub, shower, and tile cleaner. Use it to clean soap scum and mineral buildup from the tub/shower area. Scum Bum is Blue Cross Certified.

Feather duster. We are well aware of the purists who insist that feather dusters only move the dust around and don't get rid of it. We do agree that dust does need to be removed during housecleaning. In some cases, this can mean wiping the dust up with furniture polish and a cloth, or washing baseboards, or vacuuming shelves. However, when performing Maintenance/PMC on a regular basis, moving relatively small amounts of dust very quickly from one (higher) level to another (lower) level where most of it is vacuumed away is a decidedly good thing. The only feather duster that works is made with real feathers — ostrich down feathers to be exact. Down feathers are full, soft, and almost spider web-like at the ends. To prevent putting more dust into the air, bring the duster to a complete stop after dusting a surface and regularly "tap" the duster on your shoe or ankle to release dust near the floor where it will be vacuumed away.

Microfiber Duster. These are sturdier than feather dusters because there are no quills that can break off and possibly scratch a delicate surface. If your company uses both feather dusters and microfiber dusters (or lambs wool dusters), use the microfiber (or wool) duster on larger, wider surfaces such as wood blinds and shutters, window sills, baseboards, fan blades, the top of the fridge and for cobwebs above you. Just be aware of the spine of the duster so that you don't tip something over when dusting.

Cleaning cloths. The best are pure cotton — white only. Notice that we call them "cleaning cloths," so as not to suggest they're rags. Your company may prefer microfiber cloths or a combination of both. If so, your directions for managing the cleaning cloth may be slightly different. Ask your supervisor. Whatever the choice, we will refer to them as "cleaning cloths" from now on. (example: "This is how to fold the cleaning cloths so they fit correctly in your carryall tray.") It's simple but important.

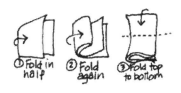

Pump-spray furniture polish. Use one that fits easily into an apron pocket.

Furniture polishing cloth. Use only for furniture polishing — not with Blue Juice or Red Juice. Microfiber cloth is ideal for dry dusting and polish dusting.

Powdered or liquid cleanser. (like Comet or Soft Scrub) Use it to clean inside tubs, sinks, and toilets. Most Cleansers can be abrasive and scratch delicate surfaces. Pro Scrub is a safe alternative for many hard surfaces.

One-pint plastic container. Use it in the bathroom to help rinse the hard-to-reach areas of the shower. It stays in your carryall tray over the top of the can of cleanser when not in use.

Whisk broom. Use it to clean the edges of carpets, especially on stairs, refrigerator grills, vents and for generalized brushing chores (e.g., between cushions on the couch).

Toilet brush. This is an example of a cleaning supply that gets worn out, even though it still has all its bristles. When the bristles are bent, they can no longer scrub at all. Replace it at that point. Avoid excess pressure when using a brush for that very reason. Use the tips of the bristles to scrub with – don't press so hard that the bristles are splayed from side to side.

Tile brush. A large brush with stiff synthetic bristles. Used to scrub the tile and grout in the shower. Also used in the tub itself and in the bathroom sink. Scrub with the tips of the bristles as mentioned with the toilet brush, above.

White scrub pad/sponge ("white pad"). Used when a cleaning cloth isn't strong enough. Carry it in a lined apron pocket so moisture doesn't get the apron (and you) wet.

Sh-Mop. The Sh-Mop uses a flat rubber surface (a full 8 by 15 inches) covered with a removable, reusable, and washable terry cloth or microfiber cover (called Sh-wipes). The Sh-Mop is three to four times faster than even an excellent sponge mop. It also gets the floor

cleaner, reaches into corners better, and cleans under the edges of appliances. The covers are tossed into the wash after use. The versa-pole collapses to a shorter size for smaller trunks. A clean microfiber Sh-wipe makes cleaning walls and wood paneling a breeze.

Floor Cleaner. Most housecleaning companies prefer liquid cleaners that don't need rinsing. Sh-Clean is one brand that is safe and effective. No rinse, streak free cleaning saves hours of time and frustration.

Ammonia. Used to clean floors if your company prefers it. You may be expected to know which floor cleaner to use on different customers' floors. Be sure to ask if you're not sure.

Vacuum cleaner—canister type. (The "Big Vac") It's easy to maneuver, it has a second turbo motor in the beater head, and it quickly separates so the hose can be used for other tasks as the need arises.

Vacuum cleaner—upright. (best for carpeted areas) This second vacuum may be necessary if you're going to work in a team because you will often need two vacuums going at the same time. Upright vacuums are easier to use if you have more carpeting than you have bare floors.

Chapter 3.

THE KITCHEN

Stock your carryall tray with the following items:
1 can of liquid or powdered cleanser
1 spray bottle of Blue Juice
1 spray bottle of Red Juice
1 white scrub pad/sponge combination (white pad)
1 pad of No. 000 steel wool (optional)
1 feather duster and/or microfiber duster
1 whisk broom
1 bottle of floor cleaner (or ammonia)
10 cleaning cloths (folded)
3 terry cloth Sh-Mop covers

Stock your cleaning apron with:
1 scraper
1 toothbrush
1 razor-blade holder with blade (optional)
2 plastic bags (as pocket liners) with clips

Hand-carry:
Sh-Mop or your choice of mop

This chapter is designed to teach you how to clean any kitchen quickly, easily, and efficiently.

The Starting Point
Lean your Sh-Mop just inside the door. Put your carryall tray on the countertop just to the right of the sink. The strategy for cleaning this room is to work around the room clockwise, cleaning as you go — never backtracking, carrying all the tools and cleaners necessary in your apron.

This room is cleaned with lots of "pick up and replace" motions. For example, pick up your feather duster, use it, replace it; pick up the Red Juice, spray and wipe, replace it; pick up your toothbrush, etc. And when we say "spray and wipe," we mean

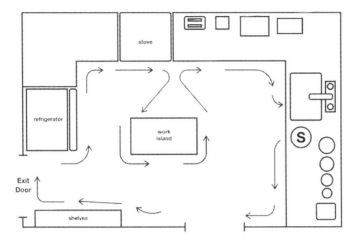

that you'll be using a cleaning cloth and the Red or Blue Juice. These motions will become smooth and effortless with practice. We've picked your starting place for you: where you put your tray.

We've drawn the floor plan for a sample kitchen and shown your trajectory through the room. "S" is where you start, and your path is indicated with arrows.

Getting Dressed
Fasten your apron around your waist tightly. Check to be sure that the toothbrush and other tools are in their proper pockets. Hang the Blue and Red Juice by their handles on your apron loops on the appropriate side. By "appropriate" we mean that if you put the Blue Juice on the left side, then 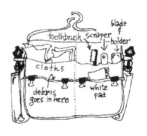 *always* put it on the left side. This is so you can quickly reach for your Red or Blue Juice without stopping to see which is which. It saves time. The tops of the spray bottles have an annoying tendency to come loose at the worst possible moments, spilling the contents everywhere. Avoid this potential catastrophe by automatically tightening the tops when you first pick them up. Stick your feather duster and/or microfiber duster in your back

pocket. Put a whisk broom in your other back pocket. Use it to brush dirt out of vents, corners, and away from walls and appliances that the vacuum doesn't reach. Estimate the number of cleaning cloths you'll need and transfer them from the tray to your apron. At first, just guess by grabbing eight to ten cloths; as time goes on, you'll know how many you need. Finally check the illustration of you and your fully loaded apron. You're ready to move on.

Setting Up
Put any trash containers just outside the door or in the doorway, making sure they are out of the way (as much as possible) of the team member who will empty it. (Follow these directions even if you're working alone, since it is work you will do later and you want these items out of your way now.) Also, lay any throw rugs outside the door flat on the floor or carpet. That's *flat*: F-L-A-T. No corners tucked underneath. No rumpled mess. You're expecting the person vacuuming to do the rug, so don't slow him down with a rumpled rug. Similarly, the person collecting the trash is not going to take the time to rummage around the kitchen on your behalf. That's your job as the Kitchen Person. If you save someone else on the team a step, you are saving yourself a step.

Cupboards, Counters and Fingerprints
You are now going to start cleaning your way around our sample kitchen, *moving to the right, working from high to low and from back to front* as you go. Get in the habit of looking all the way to the ceiling each time you look up to check for cobwebs. Above the counter are cupboards, and since they are the highest, start with them. Usually all you have to clean are the fingerprints near the handles. Fingerprints need Red Juice, so grab your spray bottle from your apron loop and spray the prints lightly. Replace the spray bottle on your apron loop as you wipe the area dry with your other hand.

You will generally be using two cloths. Carry the drier cloth over your shoulder so it's easy to reach. When that cloth gets too damp for streakless cleaning (chrome fixtures, glass, etc.) but is still usable for general wiping, hang it out of an apron pocket between uses, and sling a fresh dry cloth from your apron supply over your shoulder. If your company uses microfiber cloths, your directions for managing the cleaning cloths may be slightly different. Ask your supervisor.

Cleaning fingerprints is a task where we are careful to apply Rule 4: "If it isn't dirty, don't clean it." If all you need to do is remove a fingerprint or two from an otherwise clean cabinet door, just spray the prints and wipe dry. It only takes about five seconds. Don't haphazardly spray a large area of the cabinet door (which takes longer) and then have to wipe this larger area dry (which takes longer still). You've forgotten that all you wanted was that fingerprint and now you're cleaning the entire door. Stay focused on what you're doing, which is only the five-second job of a quick spray-and-wipe of a few fingerprints.

The places that often *don't* need cleaning are the vertical surfaces of the kitchen (the front of the cabinets, for example). The horizontal surfaces like the flat top of the counter will need cleaning every time. We have Newton to thank for this principle, plus his falling apple, gravity, and such. This is not an excuse to be lazy or to skip things that need to be cleaned. Rather, the idea is to learn to be efficient and aware of what you are doing. That includes *not* cleaning clean areas. After the fingerprints on the cabinet door, wipe the wall between the cabinets only if it has splatters. Otherwise it's not dirty, so don't clean it.

Spray and wipe the countertop area in front of you. (Pick up your carryall tray, spray and wipe the counter underneath it, and replace the tray.) Work from back to front, moving items to clean beneath and behind them. The "items" we're talking about are the sugar, flour, and tea canisters, the toaster, the food processor, and so forth. The spice rack may get moved to dust *behind* it, but that's all. Dealing with those individual containers is not Maintenance Cleaning, so just hit at the spice containers with your duster. Make sure you clarify with your supervisor exactly which items you are expected to clean during a Maintenance job.

When moving items on the counter, move them straight forward just far enough for you to wipe the counter behind them. Before you move these items back into place, now is the time to dust or wipe them. Dust them if that is all they need since that is the faster option. Now move them back, wipe the counter where they were and continue on down to the drawers below.

Be sure to dust or wipe the tops of the drawer fronts as you come to them. Always check drawer handles and knobs for fingerprints (same rule as above, for cabinet doors).

The drawer knobs or the cabinet handles are often easier to clean by using your toothbrush in the tight areas rather than by trying to fit your cleaning cloth into a small or awkward place. The toothbrush is in your apron and is perfect for corners and other areas difficult to clean with a cloth alone. Use the toothbrush and your Red Juice, and then wipe dry. After you've cleaned them with the toothbrush, a quick wipe with a cloth will suffice for many future cleanings. As you work your way around the kitchen, you will do a lot of spraying and wiping, spraying and wiping. Usually you can do this with the spray bottle in one hand and a cloth in the other.

When cloths get too wet or soiled, put them in the plastic-lined pocket or throw them to your carryall tray if you're a good shot. But be careful, cloths soaked with Red Juice or almost any other cleaner may leave spots on the floor.

Get in the habit of always putting the spray bottles back in your apron loops, *not on the countertop.* We know it seems faster to leave them on the countertop, but it isn't. This may seem awkward at first, but do it. It's faster and it saves time — and by the end of a couple days, it feels perfectly natural to replace the spray bottle back in the apron where it belongs after each use.

Countertop Problems

So here you are, cleaning the counter when you come to dried pancake batter or other difficult-to-remove items. More to the point, you discover that when you spray and wipe these globs once, little or nothing happens. What to do?

First of all, when you come to a little problem on the countertop you have to resort to tools with greater cleaning power. Use your cleaning cloth most of the time since it normally will clean the counter-top as it removes the Red Juice. When you encounter pockets of resistance like dried-on food, just move up to the tool of next magnitude—your white pad. (Rule 7. If what you're doing isn't going to work, then shift to a heavier-duty cleaner or tool.)

The white pad should be in your apron in a pocket lined with a plastic bag. When finished, always replace it in the same lined pocket. It doesn't matter that it gets dirty and begs to be rinsed, because you use it just to loosen dirt and not to remove it. Don't rinse it until you get to the sink. That may not be backtracking, but "forward" tracking isn't allowed either!

Spray with Red Juice and agitate with the white pad until a mess of Red Juice and reconstituted five-day-old vegetable soup appears. This is the mess you need to learn to "see through" (Rule 5). To do this you have to learn how to tell how the counter feels when you've cleaned through the goop to the surface without rinsing or wiping to take a look. If you have difficulty judging when you have scrubbed down to the actual bare surface (without wiping), try spraying a little Red Juice on a clean counter area next to the dirty area you are cleaning. By first rubbing your white pad on the clean area and then the dirty area, you quickly learn to tell the difference by touch alone.

Another example of switching to a higher-horsepower tool is when you encounter food dried so hard that even a white pad takes forever to work. Let's say drips of pancake batter have dried to malicious little bits of stone stuck to the counter. When you tried your white pad, you found that you were rubbing one micron or so off the top of the dried pancake batter every swipe. When you first encounter the problem, better to put your cloth away, grab your scraper, and scrape the batter loose in a second or two. Replace the scraper and continue along your way. Be careful not to scratch the surface: Spray the surface first and keep the scraper blade at a low angle. Remember, increase the force or strength of the tool only as necessary (Rule 7).

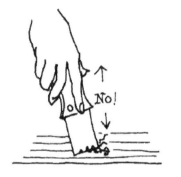

Picture Glass, Window Glass, and Mirrors
You need your Blue Juice and a dry cloth to clean these items, and since you are carrying them with you in your apron, there is no need to go back to the tray. To clean, spray lightly and evenly with Blue Juice and wipe with a dry cloth until the glass is dry. If you don't wipe it completely dry, you will leave streaks — and if you don't use a very dry cloth, you are wasting time and your energy since it will take you longer to wipe the glass dry. When we say spray lightly, we mean it. Glass or a mirror cleaned with a quick light spray of Blue Juice gets just as clean as a mirror drenched in it. It just takes two or three times longer if you overspray! So don't. Replace the Blue Juice sprayer after each use — back where it was on your apron loop.

Cobwebs and Doors
As you continue around the kitchen moving to the right,

working from high to low, look all the way to the ceiling each time you advance to check for cobwebs. When you see a cobweb, grab your feather duster or microfiber duster from your back pocket, knock down the cobweb, replace the duster, and proceed. If you can't reach the cobweb, it's likely not a Maintenance/PMC job. Check with your supervisor.

You're now ready to pass a doorway in our sample kitchen. Another place to check for cobwebs as you pass by is the top of the door frame. Did you also check for fingerprints where people (especially very little people) seem to grab the door frame as they pass through? Good.

Open Shelves
Next are some shelves used to store cookbooks, pots and pans, and other kitchen stuff. Hit at the leading edges of these shelves with your feather or microfiber duster only. This, once again, is the correct way to clean when doing Maintenance/PMC, because removing all the items from a shelf, dusting it and replacing it is often Spring Cleaning rather than Maintenance Cleaning. Ask. To clean a shelf, move all items to the right side (lifting as necessary to avoid scratching!) and clean the left side, then move everything to the left side and repeat. Finally, redistribute the items as they were. Or, if there are too many things on the shelf move just enough items to the floor or counter so there is space to move the remaining items. When moving items to the floor or counter, move them the least distance possible, being very careful not to scratch the shelf or the floor.

Refrigerator — Outside
Wipe the top first. Once you are cleaning this room on a regular basis, you may be able just to feather-dust the top, which takes only a second or two.

17

Clean the fingerprints from the outside of the fridge door — and there are always some! Don't spray and wipe the entire door unless it needs it. Clean around the hinges and the nameplate of the refrigerator — your toothbrush is the best tool. Open the refrigerator door to wipe and clean the rubber gasket. If it is dirty, make sure to use your toothbrush here also. Once you  get many areas like this clean, you won't have to clean them again for a long time: e.g., the refrigerator hinges, nameplate, rubber gasket, and cabinet and drawer handles.

Wipe the refrigerator air vent (down near the floor) while the door is open — or if it is just dusty, use your feather duster or whisk broom. While the door is open, wipe fingerprints on top and on the side of the door near the handle. Also, clean off the line left by the gasket on the inside door lining. Check for easy or obvious little wipes that are needed on the visible areas of the interior shelves. Don't get carried away — a thorough cleaning of the interior normally isn't Maintenance Cleaning.

The Stove Top
After you've cleaned the area above the stove — the hood usually needs to be sprayed and wiped — start at the back and work forward. Cleaning vent filters is not normally a Maintenance Cleaning. There are two main types of stove tops. Here is how to clean them.

Gas Ranges
These are easier to clean than electric ranges. First take the grates from the gas burners on the left side and set them on top of the grates on the right. Now spray and wipe the left side as necessary. You'll usually need your white pad here to get at the burned-on crud. If your pad won't work, use your scraper where possible, but the stove's curved edges often make this difficult.

18

If you are still unable to get the stove top clean, turn to your tray (next to the sink) and get your powdered cleanser. Use a tiny bit with your white pad. You will be using so little cleanser that you shouldn't even sprinkle it on the stove top. Instead, dab a bit from the top of the cleanser container with the wet edge of the white

pad. If there is no cleanser on the top for you to use, then sprinkle a *small* amount on the stove top and dab with your white pad to pick up a little bit. As a last resort, use steel wool instead of the white pad. Check with your supervisor before using steel wool.

After you have cleaned the left side, wipe and replace the left grates, and then move the grates on the right side to the *counter* immediately to the right of the stove. Now clean the middle of the stovetop and the right side, and replace the right grates.

Electric Ranges

Usually there is a chrome or aluminum ring around the burners that needs attention. Normally you can clean around these rings (the edge of the ring where it meets the stove top) by spraying with Red Juice and using your toothbrush around each ring. Before you wipe, use your white pad to clean the metal itself. Now wipe dry with your cleaning cloth. As usual, work from back to front and from left to right.

If you can't get the stove top clean without moving the metal rings, then go ahead and lift up that particular ring (only that one) and spray and agitate it with your white pad. If there is an accumulation under the burner, remove loose debris if you can do so without unplugging the electric burner itself. Otherwise, a thorough cleaning of a drip tray, which can take as long as cleaning the entire kitchen, is not a Maintenance/PMC item. Check with your supervisor.

The Stove Front

Now that the top is clean, clean down the front of the stove. The first little roadblock here can be a row of burner control knobs. Knobs can be cleaned by spraying with Red Juice and using your toothbrush on them and around their edges.

If you can't get this area clean without removing the controls, *first clean and wipe the knobs themselves while in place.* Then pull each one straight out, wipe it clean, and set it on the counter to the right of the stove in the same relative position it was in while on the stove. While the knobs are off, clean the area of the stove front you couldn't clean while the knobs were in place. Use Red Juice and white pad on this area and wipe it dry before replacing the knobs. This chore shouldn't have to be done every time you clean.

Open the oven door to clean the oven side of the window. It can be cleaned with your razor blade. Be sure to spray the window first with Red Juice: It's easier to clean and it's also more difficult to scratch the glass when it's wet. This window should be cleaned even though you're not cleaning the inside of the oven.

Wipe the rest of the front of the stove as necessary. Don't automatically clean the entire front of the stove. Remember that horizontal surfaces get dirty faster than vertical ones. Once again: If it isn't dirty, don't clean it.

The Middle of the Room

If there is a work island, this may be the right time to turn around and clean it. Just spray and wipe the counter top. The important thing is not to overlook it.

Toaster, Toaster Oven, Can Opener, and Microwave

Return to the last bit of counter area to

clean these items. Clean the toaster with Red Juice and your white pad, and use your toothbrush around the handles. Wipe the chrome dry and streakless (as you would glass). Clean a toaster oven similarly with Red Juice and use your toothbrush in those areas you are learning that your cloth won't reach. Also, use your razor blade on the (wet) inside glass of the toaster-oven door. The microwave is easy. Spray and wipe inside and out. Check with your supervisor regarding cleaning of other kitchen counter items such as can openers and so forth.

One important thing to know is that people don't like the housecleaners to rearrange things. It's important that you put everything you clean back in its original position when you're done cleaning the item.

A Little Reminder
Remember, don't "come back" to anything. Make sure everything has been attended to the first time around. If you have to go back to clean something you missed, you are doing something wrong, and you are wasting time—something true professional housecleaners can't afford to do.

The Sink
You will finish the trip around the kitchen by ending up in front of the sink. If there are dishes in the sink, there shouldn't be. That is not *Maintenance/PMC*. It is *daily* cleaning. Check with your supervisor.

Clean above the rim of the sink with Red Juice (not cleanser) and a cloth—all except in the bowl of the sink itself. Every time you clean, use your toothbrush around the faucets and where the sink meets the counter. It makes a vast difference and it takes only a few seconds.

Now use the cleanser in the bowl of the sink. (Use liquid or powdered cleanser *below the rim only,* or you'll spend too much time rinsing.) Conveniently enough, the cleanser is in your carryall tray right next to the sink on the counter—where you

21

left it when you started your trip around the kitchen. Wet the inside of the sink. Apply cleanser lightly on the bottom of the sink, put the cleanser back, and then use your white pad to agitate the cleanser around the bottom and sides of the sink. Use your toothbrush to clean the little groove around the drain or garbage-disposal opening.

Rinse the sink thoroughly to remove the cleanser. Use your fingers to feel the sink bottom to be sure all the cleanser is removed. Now dry the faucet spigot and handles with a very dry cloth so they will shine nicely. Put the Red and Blue Juice and the duster into your carryall tray. Take the floor cleaner and several clean Sh-Wipes (Sh-Mop covers) from your tray and put them on the counter. Set the tray just outside the kitchen door out of the path of the vacuuming.

The Floor
You may be instructed to sweep or vacuum the floor. If so, vacuum into the room so the cord or exhaust is not dragging or blowing debris. Pick up large items that may clog the vacuum —- like dog or cat food, dried lettuce leaves, carrot slices, nylon stockings, sleeping hamsters, etc. Pay particular attention to corners and to the grout on tile floors. Use a broom if no vacuum is available. (It can actually be faster, unless there are lots of dust balls around.) Your company may skip this step, depending on their policy. Check with your supervisor.

Grab the Sh-Mop from the doorway where you left it when you started the kitchen.

Mopping with a Sh-Mop
Close the sink drain and run an inch or 2 of warm water into the sink. Then add a small amount of floor cleaner into the water depending on instructions and on how dirty the floor is. Dip a Sh-Wipe in this solution. Wring out but leave it almost dripping wet, and place the cover over the Sh-Mop head. This feels a little awkward the first time, a little less awkward the next time and soon you won't even think about it. Start in the corner farthest away from the exit door and clean an area of the floor. When the Sh-Wipe is too dry or too dirty to continue, put it into

your lined apron pocket and dip a clean one in the cleaning solution in the sink. *Repeat as necessary.* This is the secret to successful cleaning of floors with any kind of mop. You must get a new Sh-Wipe or rinse any type of mop before the mop gets dry and dirty. Once the mop is dry and dirty, all you're doing is spreading the dirt around the floor instead of actually removing it. Make as many trips to replace the Sh-Wipe as necessary to get the floor clean.

As with other surfaces, different degrees of cleaning are called for: the dirtier areas of the floor in front of the stove, refrigerator, and sink require more scrubbing than less-traveled areas. As you're mopping, be prepared to use your scraper to loosen mystery globs on the floor. Use the white pad to remove smears and heel marks.

Since you don't rinse the soiled Sh-Wipes in the sink, the water stays perfectly clean. This means that a bucket is unnecessary. When you pass the sink for the last time, let the water drain, rinse the sink, and dry the chrome if necessary. Mop your way out of the kitchen. Put the soiled terry cloth covers with the dirty cleaning cloths.

YOU'RE FINISHED!
If you're working alone, it's time to start the bathroom. If you're working in a team of two, report to your partner if he/she has finished the bathroom and begun dusting. If you have finished the kitchen first, then *you* start the dusting and give your partner a secondary assignment when your partner finishes the bathroom. (See Chapter 9, Team Cleaning.) If you're working in a team of three, go see the team leader.

Kitchen Summary
(1) Lean Sh-Mop just inside door. Put tray on counter to right of sink. Hang spray bottles on apron loops. Put duster and whisk broom in back pockets and cloths in apron. Place trash cans and rugs outside. Spray/wipe around room to the right, top to bottom and back to front. When too wet or dirty, store cloths in

plastic apron pocket or throw them into tray.

(2) COUNTER: Move items forward to wipe counter behind them. Dust/wipe items and replace. Use Red Juice and cloth, white pad, or scraper on counter.

(3) REFRIGERATOR: Red-Juice outside. Open door: Clean door gasket and air vent.

(4) STOVE TOP: Clean hood, then work from back to front with Red Juice and cloth, white pad, scraper, cleanser, or steel wool.

—Gas: Set left grates on right grates. Clean left side, and wipe and replace left grates. Set right grates on counter. Clean middle and right of stovetop, then replace right grates.

—Electric: Clean with toothbrush around burner with ring in place.

(5) STOVE FRONT: Try using toothbrush and Red Juice without removing knobs. If that fails, clean knobs in place, remove and wipe them, set them on counter, clean stove behind them, and then replace.

(6) SINK: Red-Juice around rim. Use toothbrush around base of faucet. Put cleanser into bowl only and scrub with white pad. Rinse sink. Replace spray bottles and feather duster in tray. Set floor cleaner and several clean Sh-Wipes by sink. Set tray outside door.

(7) FLOOR: Vacuum with Little Vac or sweep (optional). Fill sink with 1-2 inches warm water. Add floor cleaner per directions. Dip Sh-Mop cover in solution. Wring but leave almost dripping. Put it on the mop head. Start in far corner, changing covers as needed. Use scraper or white padon problem spots.

Last time at sink, drain and rinse sink, polish faucet, and Sh-Mop your way to the exit. Put soiled covers in wash.

[NOTE: Steps 3-5 change depending on the kitchen floor plan.]

Chapter 4.

THE BATHROOM

Stock your carryall tray with the following items:
1 container of liquid or powdered cleanser (with a plastic 1-pint container
inverted over the top)
1 white scrub pad/sponge combination (white pad)
1 spray bottle of Blue Juice
1 spray bottle of Red Juice
1 toilet brush
1 tile brush
10 cleaning cloths (folded)
1 feather duster and/or microfiber duster
1 whisk broom
1 spray bottle of bleach diluted one to four with water
1 squirt bottle of tile cleaner

Stock your cleaning apron with:
1 scraper
1 toothbrush
1 razor-blade holder with a sharp blade (optional)
2 plastic bags (as pocket liners) with clips

Here is a bathroom. Looks a mess. Mold growing in crevices. Toothpaste smeared on the mirror. Crud on the grout. It looks like a big job - not at all! You'll soon learn how to clean this bathroom well using PMC techniques and be out of here in just 15 minutes or less.

The Starting Point

Walk into the bathroom. Face the tub. Put your tray down on the floor at the right end of the bathtub. The strategy for cleaning this room is to pick a starting point and proceed around the room clockwise, cleaning as you go—never backtracking, carrying all the tools and cleaners necessary with you in your apron and pockets. We've picked your starting point for you:

where you put the tray.

We've drawn the plan for a sample bathroom and shown your trajectory through the room. "S" is where you start, with arrows indicating the proper path to take.

Getting Dressed
Fasten your apron around your waist tightly. Check to be sure the toothbrush and other tools are in their proper pockets. Hang the Blue and Red Juice by their handles on your apron loops on the appropriate side: If you put the Blue Juice on the left side, then always put it on the left side. This is so you can quickly reach for your Red or Blue Juice 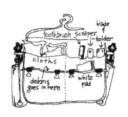 without stopping to see which is which. It saves time. (Remember, the tops of the spray bottles have an annoying tendency to come loose at the worst possible moments, spilling the contents everywhere. Avoid this by automatically tightening the tops when you first pick them up.)

 Don't put your feather duster or whisk broom in your back pockets or put cleaning cloths in your apron yet. In the bathroom, you'll be making two trips around the room instead of one: the first to do the wet work (the shower, tub, sink, and toilet), and the second to do the less-wet balance of the room.

Alert readers will notice that asking you to make two trips seems to be a violation of Rule 1. It is. Without going into a lengthy explanation, we're asking you to work like this in the bathroom (a) to avoid splashing previously cleaned areas, and (b) because you will be using brushes you normally don't carry with you. It's the most efficient way to clean a bathroom.

Setting Up
Put any trash containers just outside the door (or in the

doorway). Lay any throw rugs outside the door *flat* on the floor - no corners tucked underneath. No rumpled mess. You're expecting the person vacuuming (who may very well be you) to do the rug later, so make it as easy as possible.

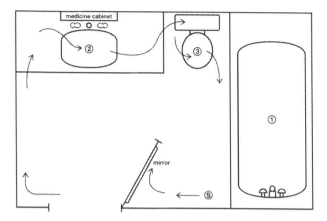

The Shower Walls

Step-by-step:
how to move
a
rubber ducky

Set any items that are around the edge of the tub out on the floor. Whenever you move items like this, move them the shortest distance possible, and keep them in the same relative position they were in. For example, if there is a shampoo container or a rubber ducky, move it straight toward you and set it on the floor in front of the tub. There are two reasons for doing it this way: (a) It is faster; (b) When it comes time to replace the items, you automatically know where they were. One important thing to know about your cleaning clients is that they don't like their housecleaners to rearrange things. So put things back into the tub/shower exactly where they were before you started the cleaning. If there's a bar of soap, put it upside down on a folded cleaning cloth on the floor. (You're keeping the soft side up so soap isn't smeared all over.) Now that we've covered how to move a bottle of shampoo, a bar of soap, and a rubber ducky, let's move on.

27

First clean the shower walls around the tub—at least the areas that get wet when the shower is on. Wet the walls using a rinsing cup or a shower wand if available. Then use tile cleaner and the tile brush. (You have two brushes—-one for the toilet and the other for the tub/shower and sink.) Although these are not in your apron, they are in your tray. And your tray (thanks to your observation of Clean Team Rule 1) is right at your feet.

Most people's arms are long enough to reach into the tub enclosure to clean - and remember the brush adds more length too. So we recommend that you stand outside the tub to clean. An effective tile cleaner liberates an extremely slippery layer of soap onto the tub floor. You can reach the shower doors in the inside by moving the doors back and forth to expose the areas that need to be cleaned. Don't squirt tile cleaner in the areas that are already clean. (The higher part of the shower wall doesn't normally get wet during a shower and therefore doesn't need cleaning very often.)

Start by squirting some tile cleaner on the wall of the shower that is farthest from the drain, and use your brush to spread it around evenly. Don't scrub. Continue around the shower, squirting tile Juice and spreading it around with circular movements of the brush. Just distribute cleaner with the brush until you've covered the area of the shower
wall that needs cleaning. Tile cleaner works mainly by chemical action, so it needs to sit there for a couple of minutes to loosen up the soap scum and hard water deposits.

If there are shower doors, continue applying tile cleaner on the inside of the doors after you've finished coating the walls. Replace the tile cleaner in your tray. Now start scrubbing the shower wall where you first applied the tile cleaner. The brush works much better than your white pad here because it digs into the grout between the tiles as well as the tiles themselves. Be prepared to shift to a white pad in some smooth showers, however. Scrub in circles from top to bottom. Clean the plumbing fixtures as you come to them, using the tile brush (and toothbrush) as needed. You'll be making a bubbly mess on the wall. Relax. It's just tile cleaner agitated by your scrubbing action, mixed with the soap and hard water deposits you are cleaning off.

"See through" this mess (Rule 5) so you can tell when it's clean underneath and can quit cleaning one area and move on to another. You do this by learning to tell the difference between how your brush feels when it is cutting through the scum versus when it is down to the clean bare surface. One way to learn this difference is to scrub a clean tile high on the wall and then scrub a dirty one. Notice the difference in friction between the two areas as you scrub. Or use your fingers on the clean versus dirty areas to be able to feel the difference.

When you come to the soap dish, clean it with your toothbrush. First scrape off the soap that has collected in the dish with the *handle* end of your toothbrush. Now brush out the remaining soap with the bristle end. Use Red Juice only if necessary. Final rinsing comes when you rinse the tub/shower area.

Shower Doors and Runners
After you have scrubbed the tile wall, continue around to the inside of the shower door. Switch to the white pad for the shower doors, as it's more effective on this smooth surface than the tile brush. (But only a white pad--never a green pad, which can scratch the glass.) Don't attempt to try to clean a shower

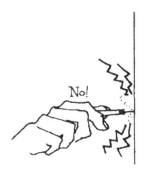

curtain, just ignore it and skip ahead. Move the doors so that you can reach inside to clean them. If the shower doors overlap and you can't clean the area where they overlap by moving the doors, then spray some Red Juice on your white pad, wrap the pad around your scraper, and slide it into the gap between the doors. (If the white pad is too thick, use a cloth instead.) Now move the scraper up and down to clean this area. Next, remove the scraper and wrap a dry cloth around it for a final wipe. The reason you use Red Juice here instead of tile cleaner is that it's a difficult area to rinse, and Red Juice doesn't require rinsing the way tile cleaner does.

It's still not time to rinse. Next, take care of the shower door tracks (runners). Usually you can clean them with your toothbrush and Red Juice. If this doesn't work, use your scraper wrapped with a cloth. Move it back and forth inside the runner to clean it. Or fold your white pad in half and push it into the runner and move it back and forth. Again, *don't rinse yet* – unless the walls are starting to get dry. It that's the case, a quick rinse is called for. There will probably be a lot of junk in the tracks, and the temptation to rinse repeatedly will be strong. Cleaning the shower runners is one of those jobs that's a mess the first time. It becomes less of a chore each time you do it, eventually needing only a quick wipe.

The Tub
Rub a dub dub, it's time to clean the tub – leaving the shower runners, the shower doors, and the shower walls clean but covered with tile cleaner and whatever else you have loosened up – all *unrinsed*. We haven't forgotten. (NOTE: If the walls and shower doors start to become dry, then you should rinse before finishing the tub.)

Wet the sides and bottom of the tub if they need it. Get the liquid or powdered cleanser out of the tray and apply it in the tub. Don't apply it anywhere but *in* the tub – not on the shower walls or faucets or shower head – just in the tub. Use the cleanser appropriately. If the tub isn't very dirty, don't use very much. While you are learning, resist your impulse to bombard the tub. Be conservative, since most cleansers are abrasives and wear out porcelain. Also, it can take as much time to rinse it away as it does to

cleaning between tile & tub

scrub the whole tub.

Use your white pad to scrub the tub, starting at the end away from the drain. Use the same "see through" method so you know when the porcelain under the foam and powder is clean. As necessary, use your toothbrush at the top of the tub where the tile meets the tub. This is often Mold Heaven (or Hell). It comes off rather easily if you can get at it with your toothbrush. The problem arises when it is found growing in the tiny cracks in the grout and can't be removed with your toothbrush. Remove what you can. Later you can use bleach on the rest, but not until you are just about to leave the bathroom, since chlorine bleach is obnoxious and you don't want to breathe it if you can help it.

Rinsing the Shower and Tub
Now everything inside the tub/shower area is a clean but foamy mess, and you are ready to rinse. Put your *unrinsed* tile brush and white pad in the sink, and leave them there while you rinse the tub/shower area.

Turn on the shower to rinse. Use cold water so you don't fog everything up. If there is a detachable shower head on a hose, rinsing is a pleasure. Completely rinse the walls and doors before you rinse the tub. Rinse the shower *walls* from front (starting above the drain end) to back and from top to bottom. If there are areas that you can't reach with the shower spray, first try using your hand to deflect the spray to the area you need to rinse. If you still can't get it all rinsed, then use the plastic container that was over the top of the cleanser to catch water and throw it to those last nasty unrinsed spots.

After the walls are rinsed clean, rinse the tub—this time back to front toward the drain. Use *your fingers* to feel the bottom of the tub to know when all the cleanser is rinsed out. Don't depend on sight alone, as it is impossible to see a little leftover cleanser in a wet tub. The reverse, of course, is also true: If you leave a tiny bit of cleanser in the tub and wait for it to dry, it makes a powdery film that will cause the customer to complain.
After you have rinsed the tub and there is no leftover cleanser or tile cleaner, turn off the water. Don't replace the items from

around the tub yet, because if there's any mold left you will spray it with bleach in a few minutes. But now is the time to wipe the chrome dry and shiny in the tub/shower area.

The Sink — Inside

Reach into the sink where you set your tile brush and white pad. Rinse the tile brush and put it in your carryall tray. Wet the bowl of the sink. Since the white pad is still full of cleanser from the tub, use it as is to clean the sink. Be careful to keep the cleanser only *inside the bowl* of the sink, since it is difficult to rinse away. *Never* let cleanser get onto an area that is hard to rinse . . . especially the top ledge of the sink around the faucets.

When the sink is clean, rinse out your white pad in the sink and put it back in your apron pocket. Rinse out the sink. You haven't touched the sink rim or faucet yet because you will do that on the second trip around the room. Grab the toilet brush and cleanser from your tray.

The Toilet — Inside

Apply cleanser in and around the sides of the toilet bowl. Wet the toilet brush by dipping it in the toilet and apply additional cleanser on it. Start high in the bowl, on the inside upper rim. Move the brush in a circular motion and clean as deep into the bowl as you can. The water will quickly become cloudy, so be sure to start at the top and methodically work your way around and down the bowl. As you wash the toilet bowl, you are also washing and rinsing the toilet brush free of the cleanser you originally sprinkled on it. Shake excess water into the bowl and replace the brush. Flush the toilet. That's out of the way!

The Second Trip

Now it's time to clean around the room. Stick your feather duster and/or microfiber duster plus the whisk broom into your back pockets. Estimate the number of cleaning cloths you'll need and transfer them from the tray to your apron. At first, try grabbing six to eight cloths. As time goes on, you'll know how many to use. You're ready to move on to the easy part of cleaning the bathroom.

You will generally be using two cloths. Carry the drier cloth over your shoulder so it's easy to reach. When that cloth gets too damp for streakless cleaning (mirrors, chrome fixtures, glass shelves, etc.) but is still usable for general wiping, keep it hanging loosely out of an apron pocket between uses, and sling a new dry cloth from your apron supply over your shoulder. If your company uses microfiber cloths instead, your directions for managing the cleaning cloth may be slightly different. Ask your supervisor. Throw your old cloth to the floor near your tray. If there's any danger of damage to the floor or carpet, put the soiled cloths in your tray.

Mirrors

Start at the right of the tray, cleaning your way around the room, moving to the right and working from back to front and from high to low. Be sure to close the door as you go by. There is often a mirror on the inside of the door, and it may need to be cleaned, so train yourself to check in each bathroom you clean. You need your Blue Juice and a dry cloth to clean a mirror, and since you are carrying these items with you in your apron, there is no need to go back to the tray.

If the mirror needs cleaning, spray it *lightly* and evenly with Blue Juice and keep wiping with a *dry* cloth until the glass is *dry*. People who have trouble with streaks leave the mirror slightly damp. If you wipe it completely dry, you'll eliminate streaks. Replace the Blue Juice sprayer after each use — back where it was on your apron loop. The mirror may NOT need cleaning — it's a vertical surface after all. Be sure to check before you automatically start cleaning it.

Fingerprints

The door also may have fingerprints on it that need a quick spray-and-wipe. Fingerprints need Red Juice, so reach for it, spray the prints, replace the bottle, and wipe the area dry.

Here's a task where we are careful to apply Rule 4: "If it isn't dirty, don't clean it." If all you need to do is remove a fingerprint or two from an otherwise clean door, just spray the prints and wipe dry. It only takes about two seconds. Don't haphazardly spray a large area of the door (which takes longer) and then have to wipe this larger area dry (which takes longer still).

The places that often *don't* need cleaning are the vertical surfaces of the bathroom (the front of the toilet tank or the outside of the tub, for example). However, the horizontal surfaces (shelves or the top of the toilet tank, for example) will need cleaning every time.

Cobwebs

Train yourself to look all the way to the ceiling to check for cobwebs each time you advance. Spiders seem especially to like corners. When you see a cobweb, grab your duster from your back pocket, knock down the cobweb, replace the duster, and proceed. If you can't reach the cobweb, check with your supervisor.

Towels

Towel racks often need your attention — especially where the towel rack is attached to the wall. This is a place to use your toothbrush. A quick swipe with the toothbrush can clean such places much faster and better than your cleaning cloth alone. Also clean the corners of the towel racks using your toothbrush and Red
Juice, and then wipe dry. Do this without disturbing any towels hanging on the rack. After you've cleaned them with the toothbrush, a quick wipe with a cloth will suffice for many future cleanings.

The Medicine Cabinet

Wipe the very top with a cloth and then clean the mirror. If it has an outside shelf (usually with a supply of bathroom things on top of it— deodorant, toothpaste, perfume, etc.), move all the items to one side and spray and wipe the cleared area. (If the shelf is too crowded to merge the two halves, move the items to a nearby countertop.) Now pick up each item and wipe it clean as you move it to the other side. Then spray and wipe the second side, and finally redistribute the items as they were. Don't open and clean the inside of the cabinet itself, as that's not part of Maintenance/ PMC.

The Sink—Outside Only

When you come to the sink, use the Red Juice to clean around the faucets and the rest of the outside area of the sink—all but the inside of the sink itself (it's already clean, remember?). *Don't use liquid or powdered cleanser!* Use the toothbrush around the base of the faucets each time. Use your white pad and Red Juice around the rest of the outside of the sink. Then wipe as usual. Use a dry cloth for a final wipe and shine of the chrome sink fixtures. Unless your supervisor tells you otherwise, don't dry the whole sink . . . just the chrome.

Debris

Check below the sink and around the cabinet for fingerprints. Continue around the bath to the right, working from top to bottom. Pay particular attention to plants (dust them and then remember to put the duster back in your rear pocket), windowsills, pictures, moldings, etc. Don't miss any reachable light fixtures in the room. As you encounter loose trash, dump the debris into the plastic-lined pocket of your apron. (Don't walk to the trash can.)

The Toilet – Outside

When you come to the toilet itself, start at the top of the tank and work down using Red Juice and a cloth. Once again, Clean Team Rule 4 applies: "If it isn't dirty, don't clean it." If the front of the toilet tank isn't dirty, don't take the time to "clean" phantom dirt. However, don't forget to wipe the flushing handle as you go by.

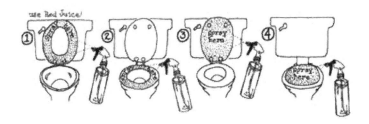

When you get to the seat and lid, put them both in the "up" position and follow this sequence carefully. After you've done it a couple of times, you'll find that the explanation is much more complicated than the doing. Use your Red Juice.
1. Spray the underside of the seat, and lower it.
2. Spray the top of the seat. Don't wipe yet.
3. Spray the underside of the lid, and lower it.
4. Spray the top of the lid. Also spray the hinges and the small flat area of porcelain on the far side of them.

Hang your Red Juice on your apron loop and wipe in the reverse order that you sprayed. That means you start with the small porcelain area and hinges. Now start using your toothbrush where needed. The first target is around those hinges. Then wipe the porcelain, the hinges, and the top of the lid dry. Raise the lid.

Use your toothbrush around the rubber bumpers and hinges (again). Wipe clean and dry. Be careful about splattering the clean porcelain. Wipe the top of the seat and raise it. Use the toothbrush again where needed and wipe dry. You're done with the lid and seat.

Now spray the top porcelain rim of the bowl. Tilt the seat and lid half forward with one hand and with the other retouch the

36

hinge area of porcelain (catching any splatters). Push the lid and seat back fully upright and wipe the rim clean.

Clean all the way down the outside to the floor, using the toothbrush on areas such as where the toilet meets the floor and around those annoying little plastic caps. (You've already cleaned the inside of the toilet so don't touch it at all.) If there is mold left at the base of the toilet after you've cleaned this area, leave it and spray it with bleach later — only if there is no carpeting involved, of course. Your supervisor may very well want you to dedicate a toothbrush exclusively for use in the bathroom.

The Floor Around the Toilet
Even though you haven't started to clean the floor yet, we prefer to be on our hands and knees, eyeball to eyeball with the toilet, only once. So clean the (uncarpeted) floor around the base of the toilet while you're there. Spray the floor around the entire base of the toilet with Red Juice and wipe it clean and dry. Remember that you have been throwing the cloths into a plastic bag (never set dirty clothes on carpet), or into your tray--as they get too soiled or wet. You can use these already-used cloths to wipe the floor. Also remember not to throw soiled cloths on carpets or wood floors — they might stain. If you have a carpeted bathroom, use the whisk broom in your back pocket to brush the areas of carpet that the vacuum can't reach.

Shower Doors — Outside
Just before you finish your trip back to where you left your tray (on the floor at the right end of the tub) you will pass the shower doors. Clean the *outside* only with Blue Juice. Often all you need to clean are the fingerprints around the handle. The outside of the tub occasionally needs a quick swipe. You're just about done!

The Floor
Take several already-used cloths to

37

do the floor. Go to the far corner and (on your hands and knees) start spraying and wiping with Red Juice as you back out of the room. The proper technique is to spray an area about 2 feet square lightly and evenly so that hairs and dust don't fly around. Then wipe up with your loosely folded cloths in a deliberate, methodical side-to-side movement (sort of a flattened "S" pattern). As you pick up hair and debris, carefully fold the cloth to trap the debris you've collected so far and continue.

When one cloth is too dirty or full, use another cloth. You don't have to dry the floor, but wipe it and turn your cloths often to avoid making streaks.

When you come to the rubber ducky and bar of soap on the floor, you can put them back around the tub, provided there isn't mold left around the tub or shower. If there is, you'll treat it with bleach in a minute, so hold off replacing the ducky and soap until the treatment is finished.

After you've cleaned your way to the door, you can bundle the dirty cloths into a "ragamuffin" so you won't leave a trail of cleaning cloths and debris on the way out of the house later. To make a ragamuffin, spread one cloth on the floor and put the other cloths in the middle. Then tie opposite corners of the flat cloth together two at a time. Presto! A ragamuffin. And you're done with the floor.

Bleach
Now is the time to apply bleach to any remaining mold still clinging for dear life in the bathroom. First make sure the window is open. Bleach destroys just about everything, so treat it like Strontium 90. Hold a cloth under the spray nozzle to catch any drips.

Set the spray adjustment of your bottle to "stream" instead of "spray" so you minimize the amount of bleach in the air that you might inhale. Apply it as a liquid dribble directly on moldy areas. Wipe off any bleach that gets on the chrome fixtures. Bleach dripping off chrome turns the tub's porcelain black. The discoloring isn't always permanent, but it can cause a customer complaint. When through, drape the same cloth over the spray nozzle to catch any drips as you take your tray through the house. One drip on a carpet will make a little white spot that lasts forever and can cost your company plenty if the carpet has to be replaced! Keep the top of the bleach spray bottle covered with a cloth at all times except when you're using it. Also aim the nozzle toward the center of the tray. Changes in room temperature can make bleach ooze out, so can pressure from other objects in your tray. The first time you dribble bleach on a carpet, you'll realize we were not being too fussy, but it will be too late.

Replace the covered bleach bottle in your tray and set the tray outside the bathroom. It's not necessary to leave bleach on surfaces for more than a few seconds. Once you've applied the bleach, you can now rinse it away.

After rinsing the bleach, replace the rubber ducky and any other items you had removed from the shower and tub. If it needs it, re-dry the chrome quickly to put the finishing touch on the bathroom.

Don't move the trash or the carpet that you previously set outside. They will be taken care of after the carpet is vacuumed and it's time to empty the trash.

YOU'RE FINISHED!

Spare Bathrooms
If there is a second bathroom that is used daily, go clean it now in exactly the same way. If there is a spare bathroom not often used, clean it according to the "If-It-Isn't-Dirty-Don't-Clean-It"

rule. Assess and use only as much energy as needed. Don't automatically clean the mirrors if they're not dirty. Don't spray the door for fingerprints if none exist. Dust items that you might normally wipe. If the tub/shower hasn't been used since you or someone else last cleaned it, just wipe it quickly with a damp cloth or spray and wipe with Blue Juice to remove dust. If you do this, it will be just as clean as the one that is used more often, but it will take you only a couple of minutes.

Different Bathroom Floor Plans
If there is a shower stall only and no tub, then treat the shower stall as you would the tub. In other words, set your tray by the right side of the shower when you first enter the bathroom.

If there is a tub separate from a shower stall, start by setting your tray down as we just taught you. Then clean the tub, the shower stall, the sink (inside), and the toilet (inside). Finally, clean around the room as previously discussed.

Bathroom Summary
(1) Put tray on floor at right end of tub. Put trash cans and rugs outside the room. Load up apron, but don't carry duster or whisk broom yet. Make two trips around the room: the first for Steps 2-6 (the wet work) and the other for the rest (the less- wet work).

(2) SHOWER: Set loose items on the floor in their relative position so replacing in the same place is possible. Put wet soap on a cloth on the floor. Wet shower walls. Spread (don't scrub) tile cleaner evenly with tile brush starting with the wall farthest from the drain and ending with inside doors. Switch to white pad for shower doors. Replace tile cleaner in tray. Start with first wall and scrub all surfaces with tile brush from top to bottom. Clean door tracks with Red Juice and the toothbrush or white pad.

(3) TUB: Wet tub and apply cleanser. Scrub with white pad, starting away from the drain. Put un-rinsed brush in the sink.

(4) RINSE: Rinse shower walls top to bottom, starting near the drain. Rinse tub starting away from drain. Shine chrome.

(5) SINK (INSIDE): Use tile brush on the inside of the bowl only. Rinse it and the brush and return brush to the tray.

(6) TOILET: Clean inside the toilet bowl with cleanser and toilet

brush. Flush toilet and rinse brush.

(7) Put feather duster and whisk broom into back pockets. Add six to eight cloths to apron pocket. Start second trip around room.

(8) SINK (OUTSIDE): Spray/wipe faucet, rim, and front of sink. Shine faucet with a dry cloth.

(9) TOILET (OUTSIDE): Spray/wipe tank. Raise lid and seat. Spray underneath the seat and lower it. Spray top of seat. Spray underneath the lid and lower it. Spray top of lid and behind it near the hinges. Wipe in reverse order. Spray/wipe rest of toilet and floor near base. Continue your way around the rest of the room.

(10) FLOOR: Spray/wipe the floor with Red Juice and already-used cloths, making large "S"-shaped movements from side to side as you work toward the door.

(10) BLEACH: Dribble bleach on areas that are still moldy after cleaning. Immediately wipe off bleach that dribbles onto metal surfaces. Rinse off remaining bleach with cold water. Dry plumbing fixtures if wet. Replace soap and other items.

[Note.—Steps 8 and 9 will be different orders in different bathrooms.]

Chapter 5.

DUSTING

Stock your carryall tray with the following items:
1   spray bottle of Blue Juice
1   spray bottle of Red Juice
10 cleaning cloths
     vacuum attachments
1   duster
1   whisk broom
1   bottle of furniture polish
1   polishing cloth
1   spare vacuum belt
1   spare vacuum bag

Stock your cleaning apron with:
1   scraper
1   toothbrush
1   razor-blade holder with a sharp blade (optional)
2   plastic bags (as apron liners) with clips

Definition
The Duster's job is to start cleaning the house except for the kitchen and bathroom. This work is drier than the work in the kitchen and bathroom: less spraying and wiping. There are several rooms involved, but they go faster, and there are no floors to wash—except wiping up an occasional drip of something. If you're going to work in a team, the Duster is also the team leader. We'll talk about that in **Chapter 9.**

Strategy
The strategy here is similar to the one for the kitchen and bathroom: Start in one place and then work your way through the rooms without backtracking, using The PMC Rules.

As before, work from back to front and from high to low. For the Duster, this instruction takes on additional importance: dust follows a relentless gravitational path downward, diverted only temporarily by air currents. Unless you have a healthy respect for this physical reality, you will find yourself redoing your work constantly. You will have an understandable human impulse first to dust what's right in front of you or what's interesting or what's easy to reach. Instead, train yourself to look *upward* toward molding, tops of picture frames, and light fixtures first, always checking for cobwebs.

Finish each area as you pass by. Do all the dusting, polishing, wiping, brushing, wet-cleaning, and tidying you need to do in an area as you pass through it. Change tools and cleaning supplies as needed. If you are dusting happily along with your feather duster and happen upon raspberry jam smeared on the top of the TV set, *quickly,* pop the duster into your back pocket with one hand as you reach for the Red Juice with the other. Spray with one hand as the other reaches for the cleaning cloth. Wipe with one hand as the other replaces the spray bottle on the apron loop. Then replace the cloth with one hand as the other hand reaches for the duster, and you are on your way again. A true blitz—a sign that you are mastering what you are doing. Don't go around the room once to dust, once to polish, once to tidy things, etc. As mentioned much earlier in your training, PMC is a very specific set of movements. You are not allowed to backtrack or randomly hop around the room.

Whether or not you are working with others, part of your strategy is to reduce the work load of the vacuumer. (The vacuumer will normally be someone else if you are working with another person.) Throughout this chapter, we'll suggest ways you can shorten vacuuming time by doing what would have been some of the vacuumer's work as you dust your way through the house.

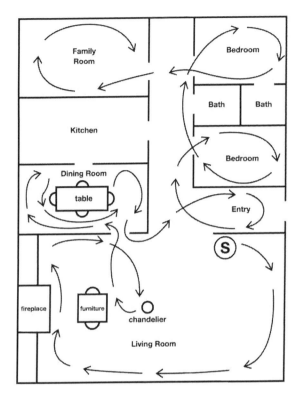

Pay attention. Be alert to smarter ways of doing what you're doing. When you shave off a minute or two each time you clean—not by rushing, but by cleaning smarter —that's what it's all about - getting more done in less time.

The Floor Plan

Since every home or apartment is unique, and since there are so many possible floor plans, we are going to discuss a typical one. Then after you've read this chapter, you'll know how to plan your cleaning through any home. So, before you even pick up your duster, you'll know where you're going to start, where you're going next, and where you'll finish.

First, though, we'll work our way through the rooms a Duster is likely to encounter—in this case, in our sample home. As we go, we'll explain cleaning methods and techniques to be used in each room and on the furniture, fixtures, and other items. Since there are so many possible arrangements, we do not suppose we're covering them all. We believe however, that by learning the correct techniques for these typical rooms you'll know how to approach items not specifically mentioned here or items arranged in a different order. We know this because it is much more important that you follow the *PMC Rules* we're teaching rather than learn "hints" about specific items. You use the same technique on a $5,000 Baccarat crystal centerpiece as on a $5 garage sale vase. You may breathe a little differently too, but you clean them the same way.

Warning:
As duster, you will be touching many items in each home you clean. This increases the chance that you might have an accident. Please be careful.

Our sample living room, dining room, entryway, and hall have rugs on a hardwood floor. The bedrooms have wall-to-wall carpeting.

Getting Dressed
Put your apron on and load it from your tray, putting Red Juice on one side and Blue Juice on the other. Put the furniture polish and polishing cloth in your apron. Put your duster in one back pocket and the whisk broom in the other. Take six to eight cleaning cloths and put them in the apron. (Next time you clean, you'll know better how many cloths to grab.)

Managing Cleaning Cloths
As you start to spray and wipe your way around the room, carry the drier cleaning cloth over your shoulder so it's easy to reach. When that cloth gets too damp for streakless cleaning (mirrors, picture glass, etc.) but is still usable for wiping, rotate it so it's hanging from an apron pocket and sling a new dry cloth from your apron over your shoulder. Use the damp cloth for wetter

cleaning jobs like fingerprints, spots on the floor, and window sills, for example. When that cloth in turn gets too damp or dirty and is no longer usable even for wiping, store it in the bottom of your lower right apron pocket. If your company uses microfiber cloths instead, your directions for managing the cleaning cloth may be slightly different. Ask your supervisor.

Managing the Feather Duster and/or Lambs Wool Duster

Approach most situations with your duster in one hand and the other hand free. Shift quickly to heavier-duty cleaning options as the situation demands, and gradually you'll notice you're beginning to do so smoothly and to anticipate your next move.

If you use proper technique with the duster, you will move most dust quickly from wherever it was to the floor, where it will be vacuumed away. (High to low—Rule 3.) Poor technique will throw a lot of dust into the air and contribute to the poor reputation unjustly suffered by unskilled dusters.

 Most dusting motions are fast, steady motions over the surface being dusted—a picture frame, for example. At the end of the dusting motion (i.e., at the end of the picture frame), bring the duster to a dead stop. *Don't let the feathers or microfiber duster flip into the air at the end of a stroke, thereby throwing all the dust into the air, where it will stay until you've finished cleaning and then settle back on all the furniture you've just finished cleaning. Remember – clean it once.* In addition, you may get a customer complaint because the dust resettled and it looks like nothing has been dusted!

By coming to a dead stop at the end of each stroke, you will give the dust a chance to cling to the duster. To remove the accumulated dust, tap the duster smartly against your ankle, close to the floor, regularly. The object is to get the dust to settle on the floor where it will await vacuuming.

One difference with a microfiber duster is that there is a stick in the middle of it, so be careful to avoid tipping something over that you're trying to dust. The microfiber duster is particularly good for larger, flat surfaces. The microfiber can also hold more dust in it than the feather duster. For this reason, it may not be as necessary to tap the duster against your ankle as often as with a feather duster.

The Starting Point
Set your tray on the floor next to the door of the first room you're going to clean. On our floor plan, the starting point is shown by an "S" in a circle. In this example, you're going to start by cleaning the living room. This starting point may change with a 2-level home. As with the "top to bottom rule" it's usually a good idea to start on the 2nd floor and work your way downstairs to the 1st level.

The Living Room

Cobwebs
Rule 3 says to work from top to bottom, so the first thing to do is to look up and check for cobwebs. Use your duster to remove them. If they're out of reach, check with your supervisor. He or she may authorize a special trip around the room with an extension duster.

Fingerprints
Dust door panels or trim with the duster. Clean fingerprints around the doorknob with Red Juice (spray and wipe). Then, with Red Juice and cloth still in hand, clean the light switch next to the door. Move to the right along the wall, dusting everything from cobwebs on the ceiling to dust on the baseboards with long "wiping" motions of the duster. Remember to stop dead at the end of each swipe with a duster. Shift to wet cleaning (Red Juice, Blue Juice, or polish) only if you need to — as Rule 7 says.

Mirrors and Pictures
Picture glass typically needs wet cleaning only a few times a year. To test for cleanliness, run your *clean* and *dry* fingers lightly over the glass. Any graininess or stickiness means clean it. If it

47

needs it, wet-clean by spraying Blue Juice lightly and evenly and then wiping dry. When we say lightly, we mean *lightly*. Besides taking more time to clean the glass when you overspray with Blue Juice, you can also cause damage if moisture reaches the bottom of the frame and is wicked up into the art behind the glass. In fact, you could ruin it! Spray lightly! Wipe it really *dry*, not just until it looks dry. The difference equals a streak: Glass begins to *look* clean as you're wiping it even though it's still slightly wet with Blue Juice. Wipe until it's completely dry. Trust us.

Wipe in broad movements, taking care to wipe the corners as well. Don't wipe in small circles or random excursions. Also, stabilize the frame with one hand — *firmly,* don't be halfhearted — while you wipe with the other. If you don't stabilize it, it may fall or leave scratches on the wall from the frame jiggling as you clean it. Don't push your luck, o.k.?

The world is full of people who can do a slow and mediocre job of cleaning glass. We want your goals to be higher, and one of the things that makes the greatest difference is checking your work. If you look head on into the glass, you will see a reflection of your own sweet face but you may miss 80 percent of the dirt on the surface. Check it from as narrow an angle as you can.

Once you have cleaned a picture frame or mirror, it probably won't need a thorough wet-cleaning again for weeks or even months. Dust it every week or so on the top of the frame and occasionally even the glass itself.

Wall Marks

As you dust, check the walls for marks and fingerprints. Use Red Juice on wall marks of all kinds. Before you move to the next section of the wall, look all the way to the floor (especially when there is a wood or tile floor) to check for little dried-up spills that should be wiped away.

End Table — Surface

Clean *above* the end table first. With wiping motions of the duster, dust the lamp shade, bulb, lamp, and then the objects on the table. If you're using a microfiber duster, be careful. Dusting such items can break the bulb or tip over the lamp. The surface of an end table is rarely touched, so there is no need to use furniture polish every week. Just use your furniture polish cloth without extra polish.

End Table — Objects

When cleaning an object-laden table, just work from top to bottom again. Use your feather duster first (on lamps and objects on the table), then a cleaning cloth (on objects that need more cleaning) and then the polishing cloth on the table itself. Use caution. Cleaning and moving small items on shelves and tables is the scene of most accidents for dusters. A few guidelines will avoid most accidents: most important, pay attention to what's in front of you. Use both hands to move anything top-heavy or irreplaceable, and anything composed of more than one piece (e.g., a hurricane-lamp base with a glass lantern on top). It's almost never wise to move something on a pedestal by pushing the pedestal. Steady the top piece with one hand and grab the pedestal with the other. You usually get to make only one mistake with such things. And keep a wary eye out for heavy objects: *Do not,* oh *do not;* slide them across the surface of furniture. Scratches will follow in their path without fail or mercy.

Dust Rings

Our end table is on a wood floor, so use your duster to wipe the floor around the legs and underneath it to save time for the vacuumer. By dusting these areas where the vacuum would leave rings or where the vacuum can't reach, you are expediting that job, since the vacuumer won't have to stop to do it. If furniture is on a carpet, use the whisk broom instead of the feather duster for this job.

Couch

Fabrics vary greatly in characteristics that affect cleaning strategy. Some furniture will need only a quick swipe with the whisk broom. At the other extreme are fabrics that hair will cling to until you pluck it off like a surgeon. In the middle are a great number of fabrics that will cooperate reasonably and respond to

your whisk broom. Every so often even the most agreeable of fabrics could use a good vacuuming to remove accumulated dust. Whether you should vacuum the entire couch and/or whether you should vacuum under the cushions depends on your company's policy. Check with your supervisor.

Back to our sample couch, however, which has pet hair and cookie crumbs on it. Clean from the top down, using your whisk broom. You will be tempted to start with the cushions, as they are easiest to deal with. Resist. First, starting with the left side of the couch, whisk the crumbs and hair from the top, back, and sides. (Careful not to make work for yourself by whisking debris onto the clean end table.) Whisk down and toward the cushion.

If your company policy is to vacuum the couch or under the cushions when it's needed, here's a system to signal to the vacuumer what to do with the couch: To signal the vacuumer that the cushion tops *only* are to be vacuumed, leave a cushion overlapping the next one. The big vacuum has a beater brush that is safe for

most fabrics. You simply lift the beater brush up to the couch cushions and vacuum away. No further vacuuming is necessary as long as you have removed the hair and crumbs from the rest of the couch. Keep in mind that you want to do everything possible to make vacuuming easier. These steps greatly reduce vacuuming time.

Be careful. Vacuuming fabric with the beater brush can catch certain loose fabrics, can catch tassels or strings, can damage certain delicate fabrics, or may accelerate the wear and tear of the couch. If you prefer to avoid any risk, use the little vacuum. If the amount of pet hair on the couch demands that the *entire* couch be vacuumed, then don't whisk it at all. It can be vacuumed with the small vacuum after the dusting. The signal to remind the vacuumer to vacuum the entire couch is to stand a cushion straight up.

Plants
Continuing top to bottom and left to right, you come upon a large potted plant in the corner. Dust the plant with the duster top to bottom. On broad-leaf plants, support a leaf with one open hand while you dust with the other so the stem doesn't snap. Pick up the dead leaves, which often clog the vacuum, and put them in the apron trash pocket. Our sample plant is close to the wall and too heavy to move easily, so with a cleaning cloth, dust the hardwood floor around and behind it where the vacuum can't reach — once again, saving the vacuumer time.

Drapes and Window Frames
Next is a wall with windows. With your duster, dust the top of the drapes and curtain rods for cobwebs. Working from top to bottom, dust all the window frames. Don't use a duster on wet windows unless you want to ruin your day. (A wet duster is a pitiful sight.) Often in the winter you'll have to wipe with a cloth because the frames are wet. Then dust the windowsill.

Leather Chair
Particles of dust, sand, and grit work their way into leather and wreak havoc with the finish and stitching. The whisk broom is excellent for dusting leather furniture, especially if the upholstery is tufted and has buttons or piping. And use your toothbrush if the cracks and crevices are dirty. Keep both in hand, because with the whisk broom you can brush away particles the toothbrush dredges up. (Brush/swipe, brush/swipe, brush/swipe. . . .)

Bookshelves

Next is the fireplace wall with bookshelves on each side. Dust the top of the books if there is room, and dust the exposed edges of the shelves with long wiping motions of the duster. Remember to release the dust from the duster at regular intervals near floor level by tapping it against your ankle.

Dust very ornate objects (e.g., candlesticks) with small squiggly motions of the duster so it reaches into all the little places.

Do not dust the hearth, because you will get soot on your duster and ruin it. Leave it for the small vacuum. If the room had wall-to-wall carpeting, you would wipe the hearth with a cloth so the vacuumer wouldn't have to bring in the small vacuum just for the hearth. (See Chapter 6, Vacuuming.)

Middle of the Room

You've worked your way to the entrance to the dining room. Before leaving the living room, dust the molding on the small section of wall between the door to the entry hall and the door to the dining room. Move to the center of the room and dust the chandelier with the duster (squiggly motions).

Polishing the Table

On the carpet in front of the fireplace is a card table with four chairs that have been well used. Moving around the table, first pull each of the chairs away from the table and dust each one in turn. Do this with your polishing cloth in one hand and a duster in the other. Use the polishing cloth on the tops and arms of the chairs and the duster on the frame and slats. Leave the chairs away from the table to make it easier for the vacuumer to maneuver.

To polish a small tabletop, spray on polish in a thin and even coat. Begin to wipe immediately, because polish left in place even for a minute or so begins to eat into the finish. *Wipe in the direction of the wood grain.* This is more shrewd than superstitious. Streaks left by imperfect polishing will be camouflaged by blending in with the wood grain if you rub in that direction. Wipe with your polishing cloth folded into an area as large as your hand — not mashed into a ball — so you make maximum use of each swipe. *(Saves time.)*As you rub, the polish will spread out evenly and begin to dry. When it is almost finished drying, flip the cloth onto its back — which should be kept *dry* — and buff the finish to a shine. Make big sweeping movements to save time. When the table exceeds your arm length, spray half at a time. (The table, that is, not your arm.) Don't press down hard as you buff. It's harder work and you can scratch the surface even with polish. Finally, check for streaks and missed spots, and deal with them with the driest part of the cloth.

Dining Room
Enter the dining room from the living room and begin dusting above the doorway, working from top to bottom as always. In the first corner is a plant: Use your feather duster as you did earlier.

Mirror-top Buffet
Across the back wall is a mirror-top buffet with liquor bottles on top. Get a funnel – just kidding. Move the bottles to the right side and spray and wipe the vacated area. Use a Blue-Juice-sprayed cloth to clean the bottles as you replace them. If you encounter cigarette butts or other debris, remember to deposit then into your apron trash pocket. *Do not* walk around looking for a trash can! Clean the other side of the mirror top and continue. Our buffet sits on the hardwood floor on short legs. The vacuum can get underneath, but use the duster around the legs to prevent dust rings.

Dining-room Table
Polish the dining room table each time unless it hasn't been used at all. It saves the most time to polish half of the table, dust the chairs closest to you, polish the other half of the table, and then finish the chairs. The point is to minimize retracing your steps.

A good brushing is all most chair seats need. Don't forget to dust the chair rungs or the legs themselves if they curve outward near the tip. While you're down there, check to see if either the pedestal or crossbeams of the table need dusting too.

The Hallway

Go into the entry hall and dust in the same way, beginning above the door and working from top to bottom around the entry. Our table is unused and requires only the duster for the objects and the polishing cloth for the table. Use the duster around the legs of the table again.

Enter the hall and continue in the same top-to-bottom manner but alternately dust and wipe sections of *both walls* as you move down the hall. Unless the hallway is unusually wide, don't do one side and then the other; you waste time retracing your route.

The Bedrooms

Enter the first bedroom off the hall. Begin in the same manner, above the door, moving to the right. Depending on your company's policy, as the Duster, you are in charge of knowing which chores are to be rotated — and which rotation is to be done this time. An example is vacuuming under the bed, which may not need to be done every week but can't be ignored forever either. The same applies to heavy furniture (like the couch), and some high molding and other difficult areas to vacuum. As usual, clarify with your supervisor.

Making Beds

It is 4 times faster to make a bed with 2 people than to make it alone. So, if there are beds to be made (or changed) and you work in a team, make the beds in a team effort. Also, make the beds first, before doing any other housecleaning. By doing the

beds first, the dust created by making the bed won't settle on an already-cleaned bedroom.

Desk

The desk in our sample room is so close to the corner that the head of the vacuum won't fit - use the whiskbroom to dust and fluff that section of carpet next to the desk. (Remember, this is wall-to-wall carpet.) This will keep the carpet pile from looking dusty. Also, set any trash cans as close to the doorway as you can without interrupting your trip around the room.

Miniblinds

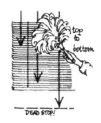

On the window are dusty miniature blinds. Lower them to their full length and turn the slats to the closed position so the blinds curve away from you. By grasping the string that runs through them, pull them away from the window so you can reach behind them with your feather duster. Dust them using long *back and forth* strokes at a slow speed so the duster can do more dust-catching than dust-storming. Remember, stop the duster dead still at the end of each stroke. Remove the dust collected after each stroke by tapping the duster against your ankle near the floor. Now turn the slats forward so the blind curves *toward* you. Dust the front in the same long, slow *back and forth* motions.

The Family Room

This room is often full and well used. This makes it doubly important that you follow the PMC method exactly.

The TV, the DVD Player, etc.

The TV is cleaned by using a duster on the back and Blue Juice on the body (of the television of course) and screen. Only dust the newer flatscreen TV's. Use your feather duster on all electronics. To remove fingerprints, spray Red Juice on your cloth and wipe them off.

Things Often Overlooked by Distracted Dusters

- Windowsills
- Molding on windowpanes, baseboards
- Chandelier chains,
- Hanging light fixtures, especially the bulbs

- Bulbs in table lamps and inside surfaces of shades
- Telephones
- Plants (dust broadleaf ones just like anything else)
- Backs of chairs
- Curved feet of chairs and tables
- Crossbeams underneath tables
- Heater and exhaust vents
- Tops of drawers and drawer pulls
- Tops of books on shelves
- Bottom shelves of anything, but especially end tables and coffee tables
- Areas around electric cords that trap circulating dust
- Drapes near the top louvered shutters
- TVs, etc.

YOU'RE FINISHED!

All that remains is the vacuuming!

Chapter 6.

VACUUMING

There May be Two of Them

If you are part of a housecleaning team, your company may use two vacuums, this makes saving even more time a real possibility.

Their Uses

Use the bigger, canister vac w/ turbo head ("Big Vac") or an upright vacuum on carpets, rugs, and some upholstery. Use the canister vacuum flat head on hardwood floors, the kitchen floor and all types of

upholstery. If you don't have two vacuums, don't worry you can use the Big Vac with different attachments the same way you would use an upright vac. NOTE: You will rarely use the small attachments when doing Maintenance Cleaning.

How to Vacuum with the Big Vac

The most important point in vacuuming is to follow Rule 1. Therefore, you plug the vacuum in once and then vacuum the entire house without ever replugging it. This little gem of an idea will save you 20 percent or more on vacuuming time by itself. You'll never backtrack (sound familiar?) to first unplug and then go looking in the next room for another plug — which is often behind the TV or couch or in some other infuriating spot.

To avoid unplugging and replugging, we use a 50-foot extension cord. The cord is stored on a cord caddy (there are many inexpensive models and styles available) that keeps it from tangling and tying itself into knots.

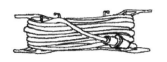

NOTE: The extension cord and caddy may not be used by your company — especially if you clean mostly newer homes that have plenty of electrical outlets.

The ideal outlet is also as close to your starting point as possible while still allowing you to vacuum the entire house without replugging. This also means that most of the cord will be *behind* you as you vacuum, which is faster than working toward the cord. Take the time to keep the cord behind you and untangled.

Take the vacuum and extension cord (on its caddy) to your starting point. Unwrap the vacuum cord and connect it to the extension cord only after tying them together in a simple knot. This is important because it will keep them from pulling apart the first time you give the cord a little tug. Next, unwrap most of the extension cord in a neat circular pile that won't turn into a giant knot later. Unwrap and lay the last section of cord in a straight line to the electrical outlet you selected. The cord in front of you is in a straight line and is much easier to maneuver out of your way, since you can move it from side to side a few inches with the beater head of the vacuum without bending to pick it up.

The above applies to wall-to-wall carpeting without modification. If there is exposed hardwood flooring, put the extension-cord pile on the hardwood floor nearest to where you will start vacuuming the rug. Otherwise you'd have to pick the pile up to start vacuuming.

Floors
Start vacuuming in the room where the Duster started, and work toward the right. Vacuum systematically, so you don't overlook an area or do it more than once. Usually you can do a living room in three fairly equal parts. Use furniture in the room as landmarks to divide the room up so you don't overlap or skip areas. Vacuum with one hand, keeping the other hand available to move furniture or other items out of your way while

vacuuming.

Typical vacuuming is a forward and backward motion. Go forward one full length of the vacuum hose each time. Move sideways one full width of the vacuum head with each backward motion. Keep the canister part of the vacuum to your left as you vacuum the room to your right. Be very careful as you pull the canister, because if an accident can happen it will.

(If you're using an upright vacuum, move forward one long step and then backward one and a half steps, because your backward steps are shorter.)

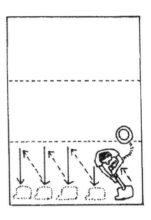

If some areas to be vacuumed are well traveled and need extra attention, vacuum more slowly or repeat each push and pull of the vacuum. If an area is little used, speed up and don't go over it twice.

Furniture

If your company vacuums the couch when doing Maintenance/PMC, please read the following paragraph. The Duster has left you signals to save time. An overlapped cushion tells you to vacuum the tops of the cushions only. Just move your beater-bar from the floor to the cushion and vacuum away. This will not harm most fabrics. But don't use the beater on very loose-fitting fabric and be careful of tassels or loose strings. (Use the small attachments.) A turned-up cushion tells you to vacuum the entire couch. You use the small attachments to do this, so leave the upturned cushion alone since that will be done later. If your vacuum has a motorized beater head, don't use it to vacuum cushions or furniture. Also, don't use the nonmotorized floor attachment, because it will transfer all sorts of fuzz from the floor to the furniture. The signal to vacuum the tops of cushions only is a single cushion left overlapping the one next to it. The signal to vacuum under a piece of furniture is when it is moved out at an angle from its normal position. The vacuumer puts the furniture back in its original position afterward.

Moving Furniture

The rule is to move the item as short a distance as possible: tip a chair back, for example, instead of transporting it. If you're helping by moving furniture as someone else vacuums, lift the item straight up, let your partner vacuum the area, and then replace it. Obviously, we're talking about light furniture that's easy to lift. If you're vacuuming on your own, you will have learned not to leave trays, mops, vac attachments, trash, etc., in your direct path. Move one end of a table an inch or two to vacuum where the legs were, and then replace.

Only if you're working in a team, it's a good idea for you *not* to replace chairs and other displaced furniture. Better to carry on vacuuming and let someone else (or you) replace items at the end of cleaning. Vacuuming is often the longest job, and every step possible should be taken to avoid stopping once you've started. For example, when you reach a spot where the vacuum head doesn't fit and an Act of Congress is required to get it to fit — like moving a heavy plant, or a desk, etc. — then this area should already have been cleaned with a whisk broom, feather duster, or dust cloth.

Stairs

Start at the top and vacuum your way down. If you have a

canister vacuum, set it six or eight stairs down from the top. When you've vacuumed down to it, move it down six or eight more steps. Use the whiskbroom from your back pocket to clean out edges and corners of the stairs as needed. It's easy and fast. Whisk several steps and then vacuum several steps and repeat. Vacuum with back-and-forth motions of the beater head — not side-to-side. Do be careful as you vacuum backward down the stairs because we don't want to lose you.

Throw Rugs

Stand on one end of the throw rug to keep it in place. Don't use back-and-forth motions. Always vacuum away from where you're standing, lift up the beater head at the end of a stroke, and start again to the right. (Move forward on a long rug and repeat the process, if necessary, until you reach the other end.) Then come back to the starting point, where you had been standing originally, and do that area from the other direction — again pushing away from you and lifting the vacuum head at the end of a push.

When finished, wrap the cord around the vacuum and the extension cord around the cord caddy.

How to Vacuum with Attachments

Unless the Vac gets a lot of use (hardwood floors, for example), use it without a 50-foot extension cord. The Big Vac has several attachments. The attachment you choose depends on whether it's being used to vacuum the kitchen floor, the hardwood floors, or furniture.

When vacuuming noncarpeted floors, point the vacuum exhaust away from the area you have yet to vacuum so you don't stir up dust. Also, pay special attention to areas where there are electrical cords on the floor. The cords trap a lot of dust and debris, so slow down and vacuum carefully.

When vacuuming furniture, follow The PMC rules: Start on the left side at the top and work your way down and to the right.

Chapter 7.

THE REFRIGERATOR

This is not a Maintenance/PMC job. However, if you are going to clean the refrigerator, do it first—before anything else. If the freezer is to be cleaned, it should have been turned off earlier so that it is defrosted and ready to clean.

The freezer is easy to clean once the ice is loose. Put any loose ice and ice cube trays in the sink and proceed to clean. If possible, don't remove anything else. Rather, move items toward the right, spray the left with Red Juice, and wipe. (If a little Red Juice gets on the frozen-food containers, it won't hurt a thing.) Now move items from the right to the left and repeat. You may have to do that in three moves or more. If the freezer is completely full, remove only as much as you have to. When you

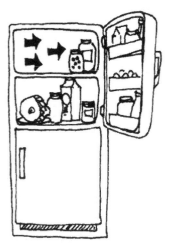 move items to make room for cleaning, move them onto the top shelf of the refrigerator.

Inside the refrigerator itself, start with the top shelf. These interior shelves don't usually need to be emptied. Items on the shelves should not be removed—just moved to the right. Then clean the racks with Red Juice and a white pad, followed by a cleaning cloth to wipe dry. If the shelves are too full to move things to the side, then remove things to the side. When only enough so you can move the rest from side to side. When you remove items from a shelf, set them on a convenient countertop or on the floor just in front of the refrigerator in the order they were removed. After cleaning, replace the items in reverse order.

Do the next lower shelf and the next until you are finished. Drawers and bins should be removed from the refrigerator because you need to clean them inside and out. Don't forget that nasty area under the bottom drawers. Crud and water both accumulate here. Generally you can clean the door shelves by removing a few items, cleaning that space, and then sliding over a few more things and cleaning under them, etc. Pick up and wipe the bottom of each item as you put it back so it doesn't leave a spot on the clean surface.

When you are finished with the inside of the refrigerator, don't clean the outside yet. Go back and start to clean the kitchen as you normally would. If you are working as part of a team, it often makes sense to have another team member do the inside of the refrigerator as you begin to clean the rest of the kitchen. The reason is that the kitchen can turn into the longest job, and you want the team to finish at the same time. (See Chapter 8.)

Chapter 8.

TEAM CLEANING GOAL
Goal

You may be working on a team of cleaners. If so, someone needs to delegate the tasks and have a good overall view of the work as it progresses. That person is the Team Leader. The primary responsibility of the Team Leader is to see that all team members finish cleaning at the exact same time.

Finally, Some Decisions to Make

To finish together requires some decision making on your part. Like where do you start cleaning so you'll finish together? When the Bathroom Person finishes his/her primary job, what's next? The same for the Kitchen Person.

The Longest Job

The key to finishing together is to identify the longest job and get it started at the right time. The longest job is the one that takes the longest time *and* that no one can help with. This is often the vacuuming.

When this longest job should be started is crucial. Get the longest job started early so it isn't still going on when the rest of the team is finished.

The graph below shows time wasted by starting the longest job (vacuuming) at the wrong time. The Bathroom Person ended up vacuuming while the other two stood idle. If the Duster had dusted only ten minutes, started the vacuuming, and then finished dusting when the bathroom cleaner had finished their primary job and was available to take over vacuuming, the whole team would have finished together. They also would finish the entire housecleaning eighteen minutes faster apiece — that's nearly one full hour less total cleaning time.

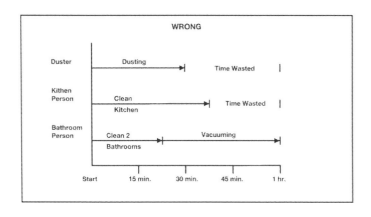

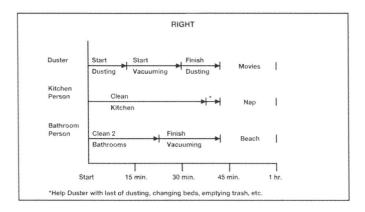

*Help Duster with last of dusting, changing beds, emptying trash, etc.

The First Time

The first time you clean a home, you should start dusting in the living room. If you later find you're unable to avoid having the team end up in the same room toward the end of the cleaning job, then change your starting point to the master bedroom.

When the Other Team Members Finish Their First Job

As Team Leader, you should ask *whoever* finished first (usually the Bathroom Person) to start vacuuming in the rooms you have already dusted. He or she should start where you did and follow your same path.

Have the Kitchen Person start vacuuming the hardwood floors (using the Little Vac), also starting in the living room and following your same path through the house. The Kitchen Person can also use the Little Vac on any furniture as signaled by you. Next, he or she gathers up the trash by going from room to room and emptying smaller containers into the largest one so only one trip outside to the garbage can is made.

Important Points: Back to Basics
We hope all of this doesn't sound difficult, because doing it is very easy:

1. If the longest job isn't finished when the rest of the jobs are, then start the longest job sooner the next time you clean that house.

2. If you all end up in the same room at the end, then dust that room sooner or vacuum it sooner or empty the trash from it sooner.

3. If the dusting job is taking too long, then have a second team member do some of the dusting.

4. If you aren't finishing together even after getting the longest job started earlier, save all the short jobs for last—emptying trash, putting throw rugs back in place, finishing touches, and checking each other's work (nicely, nicely).

5. If you still have problems finishing together, sit down and talk about it. Don't feel that just because you're Team Leader you are alone in a boat adrift. Try suggestions that come from the other team members.

Chapter 9.

TEAM CLEANING

Team Cleaning in a Team of Three or More

Most of what we've discussed in this chapter applies to a team of three. The jobs are a Kitchen Person, a Bathroom Person, and the Duster.

Team Cleaning in a Team of Two

In a team of two, one person starts as the Bathroom Person and the other as the Kitchen Person. The Team Leader is the one who finishes the initial assignment first—normally the bathroom. The Team Leader then changes the bathroom tray into a duster tray and starts dusting. The Kitchen Person starts vacuuming with the Big Vac after finishing the kitchen. Make adjustments so that each time the two of you clean you come closer and closer to finishing at the same time. It is simpler for two people to finish at the same time than three, since there are fewer possibilities for how to divide up the work.

Team Cleaning in a Team of One

This is the most efficient way possible. No decisions, no negotiations—just follow the PMC methods and you get faster every time you do it.

Recording Your Improvement

Your company will likely have you record both the start and stop time of each house you and/or your team cleans. Use this as a training tool. Observe yourself to be sure you haven't introduced some backtracking or other violations of the PMC Rules. Also observe your teammates and make sure they are also following the PMC Rules the way they were taught to do.

Chapter 10.

AN ENCOURAGING WORD

Did you ever despair over learning to tie your shoe, ride a bike, or swim? Can you remember how difficult it was to do something that is now mindless in its simplicity?

Did you ever learn touch-typing? If you did, you know that it took you longer to use touch-typing than your old hunt-and-peck method when you were first learning. You had to break comfortable, old, (inefficient) habits and replace them with new, unfamiliar, and uncomfortable (but very efficient) habits.

Also, if you used your old hunt-and-peck method of typing all day long every day, you would never, ever get much faster than 30 words a minute — even with all that practice. However, if you practiced your new touch-type method daily you would improve your speed constantly - 100 words per minute is not an unheard of speed. That's more than three times faster than a method that once seemed just fine to you.

Practice the PMC techniques exactly and you WILL get faster and better at the same time. You will truly be amazed at how thoroughly and quickly you get each house cleaned. Your co-workers will refer to you as a super cleaner and will fight over who gets to work with you! So get your duster, and keep moving. You'll do great!

Here are a few more "gems." A successful housecleaner or housecleaning team always:

- Shows up on the day and time scheduled
- Is friendly and communicates well with the client
- Leaves things in the place they were originally found
- Works efficiently and cleans thoroughly

- Takes pride in their work
- Is careful not to break anything
- Follows directions
- Accepts responsibility for accidents
- Remains loyal to their job
- Doesn't eat the client's food (unless invited)
- NEVER considers taking anything from client's home
- NEVER abuses technology on the job (non emergency cell phone use, using client's computer, posting on Twitter & Facebook, snapping photos of clients home, watching TV on the job, you get the picture….)
- Follows the proven efficient, effective PMC system exactly — every time.

What are the results of demonstrating these qualities? Superior cleaning! A happy boss! This means more money, a rewarding career and physical and mental energy to enjoy your *personal* life — but most importantly - job security.